Sound familiar?

That's because loads of people think that way - but when you're already feeling pretty bad, thoughts like these make you feel even worse.

The fact is, bad thoughts **cause** bad feelings. It's not just the other way round. So one way to feel better is to do something about the bad thoughts.

This book will show you how.

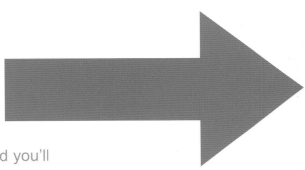

Turn the page and you'll see what we mean.

GOOD
MOVE!

You turned the page!

You didn't say "Oh, forget it!" and chuck the book at the cat - you turned the page and took a giant leap towards feeling better - by yourself.

Keep on turning and you'll find out how to *keep on* feeling better and better, with the

AMAZING BAD-THOUGHT-BUSTING PROGRAMME

Now you're going to learn to spot some bad thoughts.

LET'S PLAY DETECTIVE

Magnifying Glass at the ready?

The key to good detective work is to slow things down and be on the lookout.

Try this task to start noticing your own bad thoughts.

Imagine yourself into each situation, and try to spot the thoughts that pop into your mind.

1). You're late for an important meeting. You're stuck in traffic and can see the building you want to reach. You know you're going to be really late.

2). You invite friends round for a meal, but notice one of them doesn't eat much of it and says they're not hungry.

3). You play sport but this week you're not picked to play.

Then complete the worksheet on pages 8-9. Use the questions to help you identify the thoughts that occur. Write down as many as you notice, then turn the page to label the thoughts.

HOW TO FILL IN THIS SHEET

CHOOSE A TIME WHEN YOU FELT BAD

WHAT WENT THROUGH YOUR MIND AT THE TIME?

- ABOUT YOU?
- ABOUT OTHERS?
- ABOUT WHAT HAS HAPPENED?
- ABOUT WHAT MIGHT HAPPEN?
- ABOUT WHAT OTHERS THINK ABOUT YOU?

MY BAD THOUGHTS

BAD THOUGHT SPOTTER

Bad thoughts are also known as unhelpful thinking styles.
They are habits of thinking we can fall into time and time again.
These thoughts need tackling because:

- they worsen how we feel emotionally and physically
- they affect what we do. So, we might say
  no to something when yes could be fun.

This bad thought spotter will help you spot when your thinking isn't helping.

Look back at the thoughts you wrote down on the last two pages. Now label them using the bad thought spotter on page 11.

Are any of these thinking styles familiar? Have you been here before?

If you tick one or more boxes on the right, you've spotted a bad thought that you can fix with the Amazing Bad Thought Busting Programme.

UNHELPFUL THINKING STYLES	Tick
Are you your own worst critic? Do you always seem to be beating yourself up about something?	
Do you focus on the bad stuff? As if you were looking at the world through darkened glasses?	
Do you have a gloomy view of the future? Expecting everything to turn out badly.	
Are you jumping to the worst conclusions? It's called 'catastrophising'.	
Do you assume that others see you badly? When you haven't checked whether it's true, it's called 'Mind-reading'.	
Do you take responsibility for everything? Including things that aren't your fault.	
Are you always saying things like 'Should' 'Ought to' 'Got to'? Setting impossible standards for yourself?	

TURN THE PAGE TO BEAT THESE BAD THOUGHTS

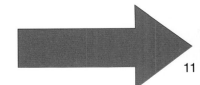

11

First, label the thought

When you notice one of your bad thoughts, don't get caught up in it, just mentally step back and stick a label on it.

"Oh that's just one of those bad thoughts"

When you label a bad thought this way, **it** loses its power and **you** realise it's just part of being upset.

It's not the truth, it's just one of those bad thoughts.

You could even talk to it. Say: "You're rumbled! I'm not playing that game again!"

Turn over for **STEP 2**

NOW LEAVE IT ALONE

Mentally turn your back on the bad thought.
Don't challenge it or try to argue with it,
just let it be.

Bad thoughts love attention so don't give them any.

Instead, think about what you're doing right now,
or stuff that you're planning for the future,
or things you've achieved lately.

STEP 3 next

STAND UP TO IT!

Don't be bossed about by bad thoughts

Bad thoughts are like bullies - they can be intimidating. But although they sound strong, really they're weak underneath. And they tell lies.

They say you won't like doing something. They say you'll fail if you try. They tell you you're rubbish or you're scared or nobody likes you.
But this is just the bad thought, not the truth.
Don't be bullied!
If the thought says "Don't" then DO!
If the thought says "Can't" say "CAN!" Right back at it.

Easy for us to say? You're right.

But if you don't give it a try you'll never know. And, just what if you really did beat those bad thoughts?

Turn over for the next step

GIVE YOURSELF A BREAK

Be a better friend to yourself, you deserve it.

Bad thoughts are how we beat ourselves up when we're upset. We often say things to ourselves that are critical and nasty – things we would never say to someone we cared for. And we often say things in such a nasty or scary tone.

So if you're having trouble with a bad thought, think what a person who really loved and wanted the best for you would say, right now. What words of encouragement and support might they offer?

They'd disagree with the bad thoughts. They'd remind you that you're not rubbish, or stupid, or bound to fail.

Trust these positive things and let them help get rid of the bad thoughts.

Turn over for **STEP 5**

HOW TO BEAT THE REALLY BAD ONES

Some bad thoughts are hard to beat.

They keep coming back and you wonder if you'll ever get the better of them.

Here are three things you can do that will help.

T

Look at the situation differently

First, imagine what it would be like if it was a friend, not you, who was having this bad thought. What advice would you give? Now give the same advice to yourself.

Put your thought or worry into perspective. Will it matter in six months? Will you even remember what the problem was? If it won't matter in six months, it's probably not that important now.

How would others deal with the problem? Think about someone who seems to handle problems well and work out what they would do, or how they would think in this situation.

Turn over to **RECAP**

SO:

THE AMAZING BAD-THOUGHT-BUSTING PROGRAMME

Bad thoughts mess you up and
actually **cause** bad feelings.
Beat bad thoughts and
you'll feel better.
When you notice a bad thought:

1. LABEL IT
Oh, you're just one of those
bad thoughts.

2. LEAVE IT
A bad thought needs attention, so
don't give it any.

3. STAND UP TO IT
Bad thoughts can be scary but
like bullies are weak underneath,and
they tell lies. You can beat them.

4. GIVE YOURSELF A BREAK
What would someone who really
loved you say? Trust them and let
them help you beat the bad thought.

5. LOOK AT IT DIFFERENTLY
Give yourself the advice you'd
give to a friend. Ask yourself if it
will matter in six months. Pick
someone you know and work out
how they would handle
the situation.

So what are you waiting for?
Let's try it out

THE AMAZING BAD-THOUGHT-BUSTING PROGRAMME

1. Label it
Oh, you're just one of those bad thoughts.

2. Leave it
A bad thought needs attention, so don't give it any.

3. Stand up to it
Bad thoughts are like bullies - weak underneath. You can beat them.

THE AMAZING BAD-THOUGHT-BUSTING PROGRAMME

4. Give yourself a break

What would someone who really loved you say? Trust them and let them help you beat the bad thought.

5. Look at it differently

- Give yourself the advice you'd give a friend.
- Ask yourself if it will matter in six months.
- Pick someone you know and work out how they would handle the situation.
- Ask yourself if it matters so much.
- Are you basing this on how you feel rather than the facts?
- What would other people say?
- Are you looking at the whole picture?

GO
FOR
IT!

Don't worry

If this seems hard at first. A good place to start is to practice on bad thoughts that are only slightly upsetting to begin with.

It takes practice to beat bad thoughts.

But the Amazing Bad Thought Busting Program really works, so keep trying and within a few days, you'll have your bad thoughts on the run and be feeling better.

Remember the key things is to plan to practice this approach.

DON'T JUST SIT THERE, MAKE A PLAN!

1. WHAT AM I GOING TO DO?

2. WHEN AM I GOING TO DO IT?

3. WHAT PROBLEMS OR DIFFICULTIES COULD ARISE, AND HOW CAN I OVERCOME THEM?

Is my planned task

Q. USEFUL FOR UNDERSTANDING
OR CHANGING HOW I AM?

YES ☐ NO ☐

Q. SPECIFIC, SO THAT I WILL
KNOW WHEN I HAVE DONE IT?

YES ☐ NO ☐

Q. REALISTIC, PRACTICAL
AND ACHIEVABLE?

YES ☐ NO ☐

MY NOTES

WHERE TO GET EVEN MORE ADVICE AND SUPPORT

Sometimes, bad thoughts feel like part of you and you just can't seem to label them, leave them or stand up to them.

That's when you need a bit more advice and support than this little book can give.

You can get it at www.llttf.com.

Having bad thoughts is part of feeling down, as is feeling tired all the time, drinking too much, self-harming, not seeing friends, being scared to go out and other problems. This little book is a companion to all the one's on the right. When you've sorted your current problem, you might want to choose another little book and work on something else in your life.